COUNTRY LIVING

BETA-PLUS

COUNTRY LIVING

January 2007
ISBN 13: 978 90 772 1364 3
ISBN 10: 90 772 1364 3

p. 4-5

A project by
Costermans.

CONTENTS

If you can keep your head when all about you
   Are losing theirs and blaming it on you;
If you can trust yourself when all men doubt you,
   But make allowance for their doubting too;
If you can wait and not be tired by waiting,
   Or being lied about, don't deal in lies,
Or being hated, don't give way to hating,
   And yet don't look too good, nor talk too wise;

FOREWORD

More and more people are choosing to escape from the bustle of city life and retreat to the countryside: dilapidated farmhouses are being restored, old country houses are being returned to their former glory and newly-built projects are integrated into the landscape. The aim is always to create a sense of harmony with the existing environment.

This book contains around twenty reports featuring all aspects of country living: from the restoration of the house and the selection of materials to the interior design and the landscaping of the garden.

Wim Pauwels
Publisher

A project by Benedikte Lecot.

p. 12-13
A project by
Costermans.

PART I

COUNTRYSIDE
INSPIRATION

A COUNTRY HOUSE IN PERFECT HARMONY WITH NATURE

Since 1970, Vlassak-Verhulst have carried out over eight hundred exceptional residential projects of the highest quality. In recent years, the company has expanded to become the market leader in the construction of exclusive homes: an ideal partner for building projects, for whom quality, professionalism and customer satisfaction are of prime importance.

Vlassak-Verhulst make the case for a timeless, classic style of construction with modest charm, perfectly in keeping with the landscape of the Low Countries.

The country house in this report is a fine example of Vlassak-Verhulst's expertise: an atmospheric country home surrounded by nature in the green outskirts of Antwerp.

The roof is clad with old blue Boom tiles and reed thatch.
Old, reclaimed paepesteen bricks laid in cross bond were chosen for the façade.

p. 18-19

The house and garden are in perfect harmony.

The main door is the real eye-catcher at the front of the house: the aged, brushed oak extends into the

window section above the door.

The bottom part of the wall is finished with a layer of pitch coating that just peeps out above the low hedge.

p 20-21
At the back of the building, a variety of windows draws the attention. To the left is the wooden corner window of the kitchen, with a large metal-framed cross window next to it. A sliding wooden door can be used to close off the window of the living room.

Lines of large, sawn-bluestone tiles give an extra dimension to the entrance hall. The sober atmosphere is accentuated by the aged-oak staircase with its brick balustrade.

A pleasant working environment, with a lot of light and contact with the beautiful greenery of the garden.

The custom-made, painted wall-unit provides plenty of storage space.

p. 26-27
Paepesteen bricks
around the open
fireplace.
The window in this living
room provides contact to
the surrounding nature
all year round.

p. 24
The floor in the living room is made of wide oak planks.

The window above the oak counter with its old sink allows a lot of light into the room.

The wall behind the oven has been clad with zeliges.

Simplicity, warmth, functionality and atmosphere in this kitchen, emphasised by the all-oak central unit that provides extra workspace.

p. 30-31
The kitchen dining area and the living room are separated by a door made of oak planks and metal frames, finished with putty. Cane chairs around a simple, spacious kitchen table.

p. 32-33
Painted wooden panels in harmony with the white Carrara marble floor and bath and washbasin surrounds.

Bathroom, dressing room and bedroom flow into one another.

Painted cupboards and an oak floor in the dressing room and bedroom.

The old oak truss reaches up into the ridge of the house.

VLASSAK-VERHULST nv

Moerstraat 53

B – 2970 's-Gravenwezel

T +32 (0)3 658 07 00

F +32 (0)3 658 46 45

www.vlassakverhulst.be

info@vlassakverhulst.be

PAYING TRIBUTE TO A RICH ARCHITECTURAL HISTORY

In this project, as in the previous report (p. 16-35), Vlassak-Verhulst reveal their fondness for the rustic style of architecture, created according to traditional methods and owing a great deal to our rich history of construction.

The harmony of house and garden is a central feature of this project as well: this country house has been completely integrated into its beautiful natural surroundings.

This Kempen country house was built with old paepesteen bricks and reclaimed Boom tiles. White shutters on the windows.

Left

The terrace around the authentic metal greenhouse (thin frames, finished with putty) is laid with old Dutch clay clinker bricks in Waal size.

p. 40-41

The large painted doors are inspired by the farmhouses of old. However, the spaces behind them no longer contain stables or storerooms, but luxurious living areas and concealed terraces.

p. 38

Old grey-brown farmyard cobbles.

A pool house in typical Kempen style with its covered terrace and old oak supports. Virginia creeper grows around the canopy.

p. 44-45
The thatched roof has been installed in a traditional, irregular style.

The shades of grey create a feeling of cosiness. The correct positioning of the windows ensures that this living room receives the right light at every moment of the day.

'Hollandse witjes' tiles in stretcher bond. A solid slab of bluestone as a work surface, finished with a contoured edge detail, and a custom-built cooking unit in aged oak.

Wooden shutters on the bedroom windows.

The radiator fits snugly under the wooden window ledge.

VLASSAK-VERHULST nv
    Moerstraat 53
    B — 2970 's-Gravenwezel
    T +32 (0)3 658 07 00
    F +32 (0)3 658 46 45
    www.vlassakverhulst.be
    info@vlassakverhulst.be

p. 48

The bathroom is clad
with small glass-mosaic
tiles. The white porcelain
washbasins have clean,
rectangular lines. The
small windows provide
abundant light, whilst
also ensuring the
necessary privacy.

THE RENOVATION
OF A POLDER FARMHOUSE

The aim of this renovation project was to make it appear as though this authentic farmhouse had just been done up. But the farmhouse actually required complete renovation, which was carried out with respect for the materials and the local style of construction.

The owners and their interior architect succeeded marvellously in achieving their goal.

On entering this house, you notice the thorough renovation work. This farmhouse is a symbiosis of functionality, simplicity and authenticity.

Natural light was an important factor in the project.

p. 56-57
It took many years of searching to bring together the furniture and objects in this home.

Open fireplaces have been incorporated in a number of locations.

p. 58

All of the construction materials used for the floors, ceilings, doors, fireplaces, staircases, and so on, are authentic items with their own history. They have been expertly combined to give the impression that they have always been there.

The spacious kitchen has been designed in a
most functional way, with a central cooker
and lots of storage space and work surfaces.

The parents' bedroom with its dressing room and
bathroom with a view of the garden.

The adjoining bathroom with washbasin blocks and a walk-in shower.

Unusual objects have also been perfectly integrated into the authentic rustic character of the house in the upstairs area set aside for the children and guests.

RUSTIC INSPIRATION

This countryside villa was designed by the Demyttenaere architectural studio from Knokke.

Sand's Company, the interior-design firm that works closely with Demyttenaere, took care of the complete interior of this idyllically situated house.

The use of thatch and horizontal planking reinforces the informal, rustic character of this villa.

Smoothed bluestone tiles were selected for the entrance hall, finished with cabochons of polished white Thassos marble.

The wall behind the fireplace is in brushed, white-oiled French oak. The fireplace has a surround of Pietra Piasentina natural stone.

In the bathroom Azul Fatima natural stone has been combined with doors in solid brushed and oiled oak. The shower has been clad with antique Megaron Lapideum marble mosaic of 5x5 cm (Botticino on net).

The cupboard unit and the wall behind the bed are in sandblasted and stained oak veneer.

DEMYTTENAERE H-C bvba
Architectural studio
    Koningslaan 160
    B – 8300 Knokke-Heist
    T +32 (0)50 62 37 79
    F +32 (0)50 62 37 80
    hcd@myth.be

SAND'S COMPANY
    Interiors
    T +32 (0)50 62 68 08
    F +32 (0)50 62 37 80

THE TRANSFORMATION
OF A DAIRY FARM

This dairy farm and its farmhouse, both of which date from the early nineteenth century, have been thoroughly restored under the direction of architect Bernard De Clerck.

This involved incorporating the old milking parlour into the house, so as to create a large kitchen and dining area.

A barn, covered terrace, pool house and mudroom have also been added.

The side of the house facing the road.

The kitchen with its large glass doors (on the extreme left in the photo), the service entrance and the barn all open onto the courtyard to the right of the house.

The oak extension in the corner of the building houses the kitchen's washing-up area.

p. 84-85

The side wall to the left of the building, covered with wisteria and climbing hydrangea.

p. 86-87

The covered terrace with the pool house, and a completely rebuilt space to the right of it, which now contains the kitchen and dining area. The large, new glass doors in the central section lend a new elegance to this side of the house.

The washing-up room next to the dining room; a view from the dining room into the living room and the hall with the staircase.

The study has been embellished with Italian baroque sections in oak.
An English desk and plaster anatomical models.

The master bathroom with its oak floor, surfaces in Massangis Roche Jaune and painted cupboards.

BERNARD DE CLERCK
Architectural studio bvba
    Aarselestraat 26
    B – 8700 Aarsele
    T +32 (0)51 63 61 39
    F +32 (0)51 63 52 15
    info@bernarddeclerck.be

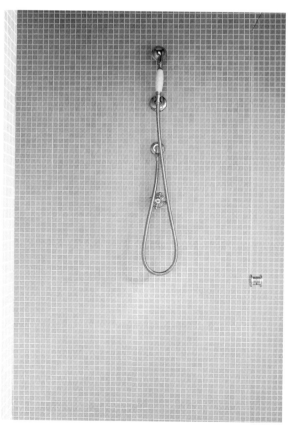

A CLASSIC VILLA
IN A BUCOLIC LANDSCAPE

Virginie and Odile Dejaegere designed the interior of this country house, which is situated in a breathtaking natural landscape, bordered by lines of pollard willows and with a view over extensive meadowland.

The garden was created by landscape architect Paul Deroose.

Classic inspiration for this stately country house, both outside and inside.

A line of pollard willows separates the grounds from the surrounding meadows.

A black Basècles church floor with white stone edging was selected for the hall. The stairs are in solid oak and have been painted. All of the door furniture was specially made by Vervloet–Faes. The wall-lights in the hall are by Stéphane Davidts. Lime paints were used for the walls.

Two old sets of double doors have been transformed into built-in shelving units with fabric insets.

The curtains are made from linen. An oak floor with planks of different widths.

Old terracotta tiles in the orangery. The planks are old, untreated pinewood.

The chair has a linen cover.

The bathroom floor, the washbasin and the bath have all been clad with Amarello Negro marble. An oak floor
was selected for the dressing room.
A Stéphane Davidts wall-light in the bathroom. The walls have been painted with a lime finish.

DEJAEGERE bvba

Virginie & Odile Dejaegere
Grote Markt 7
B — 8500 Kortrijk
T +32 (0)56 22 87 81
F +32 (0)56 20 49 93
MOB +32 (0)475 79 13 78
www.dejaegere-interiors.be
info@dejaegere-interiors.be
By appointment only

THE METAMORPHOSIS
OF A FARMHOUSE INTO
A COUNTRY MANOR HOUSE

Tradiplan, the exclusive home construction company, ensured the successful transformation of this modest farm with a small residential section and a number of stables into a charming country manor house with generous proportions.

Only the exterior walls of the original farmhouse remain standing: all of the rooms inside have been redesigned and the stables have also been equipped as living areas.

The owners, who work in the hotel sector and are passionate about interior design, have created a look that radiates both timeless class and simple rural charm.

White rendered walls, aged window frames in afrormosia wood, reclaimed tiles, steel skylights – every element contributes to the lived-in character of this country house.

The windows have been extended; the stables have been converted into living space.

Country living in an unspoiled natural landscape.

Two old varieties of marble have been laid in a checked design: small tiles in the hall and larger ones in the dining room (p. 116-117).

The wooden floors and skirting are
in reclaimed teak.
The ornamental fireplace and built-
in cupboards are in reclaimed pine.

The owners have created a very personal interior with a number of valuable antique pieces of furniture. They also attach a great deal of importance to details: the switches were inspired by old models that were often used in farmhouses.

In the kitchen, old terracotta tiles have been combined with oak kitchen units that have been clad with natural stone. The wall tiles are antique Dutch 'witjes'.

TRADIPLAN
Lodderstraat 14
B – 2880 Bornem
T +32 (0)3 889 15 75
F +32 (0)3 889 26 66
www.tradiplan.be
info@tradiplan.be

SETTING THE STANDARD
FOR LUXURY LIVING

For 35 years, b+ villas has been one of the most respected construction companies in Belgium and the southern Netherlands.
Whether it's a new-build project, a renovation or a whole interior, you can always rely on b+ villas to design, create and coordinate the entire project.

"Luxury Living" is the slogan under which this Aarschot company offers its services: the creation of exclusive, distinctive homes that correspond perfectly to the wishes of the client, whatever the style he chooses.

The two projects in this report are excellent illustrations of the company's philosophy.

This house, situated in the middle of a historic village in Waals-Brabant, consists of a central residential area, with a classic presbytery layout: a central entrance hall with rooms to the left and right and the kitchen at the back.

Two bedrooms, a bathroom and a dressing room have been created on the first floor. There is an extra guestroom in the attic.

The outbuildings have been refitted as an office space with a separate entrance. The additional living space between opens onto the terrace.

The renovation involved minimal alterations to the existing interior and exterior structure of the house.

The interior was designed by Paul Vaes of b+ interiors.

Di Legno wooden floors, old oak planks (up to 230 cm long and 19 cm wide), oiled in grey. A Stüv open fireplace. LE carpet, collection silex.

The kitchen furniture is made from melamine panels and painted MDF façades. Surfaces in smoothed bluestone with a grooved edge.

Floors in old bluestone, Cottage 40x40 cm.

A Corton (Buxy) Cottage floor was chosen for the bathroom.

This country house in the leafy outskirts of Brussels was constructed in reclaimed "Brugse mof" bricks and reclaimed grey Boom tiles. The horizon swimming pool has an overflow gutter running between the bushhammered and sawn bluestone surrounds. The swimming-pool machinery has been incorporated into the cellar of the pool house.

Reclaimed Burgundy slabs have been used throughout the entrance hall and salon.

The cooking island is topped with Jasberg granite. Irish bluestone on the floor.

b+ villas

Nieuwlandlaan 19
B – 3200 Aarschot
T +32 (0)16 56 79 31
F +32 (0)16 56 20 38
www.bplusvillas.be
info@bplusvillas.be

b+ interiors

Nieuwlandlaan 19
B – 3200 Aarschot
T +32 (0)16 55 35 60
www.bplusinteriors.be
info@bplusinteriors.be

A diagonal floor design in two types of marble: Carrara and Bardiglio.

PART II

COUNTRY INTERIORS

ETHNIC INSPIRATION IN DIALOGUE WITH CONTEMPORARY ART AND DESIGN

All of interior architect Annick Colle's projects display a fascinating blend of apparent contrasts.

She creates sophisticated combinations, mixing antique objects from distant cultures with modern design and contemporary art. The result is a serene atmosphere that radiates a sense of calm and warmth. The project in this report is a convincing illustration of her vision of design.

Annick Colle heads a studio of interior architects. She receives her clients in the informal surroundings of her own home.

Her interiors are all created in close consultation with her clients and designed with modern home comfort in mind.

A pre-Columbian wall-hanging from the area around Nazca, Peru (2000 BC).

Two armchairs in green buffalo leather beside a wengé Liaigre table.

In the foreground, two Danish stools, designed by Paul Hundevad in 1950, in black leather and rosewood, bought from Philippe Denys.

The dining room with its Hans Wegner chairs can be seen through the door on the right.

p. 138-139
A lamp by Liaigre on a console. Photo by Miguel Rio Branco.

A dark tadelakt floor. Integrated mirrored wall-cupboards and Dornbracht fittings. The surfaces are in aged Azul Fatima stone. Units in solid oak, brushed and aged.

The wall-unit and screen are made of brushed and tinted solid oak.
Bedside table and footstool by Liaigre. African textile on the bed. Night lights by S. Davidts.

In the centre, a Beovision plasma screen by B&O. The oak parquet has been given a dark tint. In the background on the left is an artwork by Jan Decock.

ANNICK COLLE
    Interior architect
    Reinaertdreef 8
    B – 9830 Sint-Martens-Latem
    T +32 (0)9 282 66 41
    F +32 (0)9 281 18 57

p. 142
The white blinds soften the light in this pool house/multi-purpose room for teenagers. The red work of art is by Anne Veronica Janssens. Corner seating-unit by B&B and a white Carrara table by Skipper.

A PERFECT BALANCE BETWEEN CLASSIC AND MODERN

Benedikte Lecot is an interior designer who aims to create a symbiosis of functionality, atmosphere, light and architecture in all of her projects.

She aims to achieve a unity of style within a pleasant living environment that balances classic and modern, and which is always in keeping with the individual needs and desires of the client.

All of her designs are therefore created à la carte.

The exclusive character of her interiors is further reinforced by perfect workmanship, carried out by experienced and passionate professionals.

Benedikte Lecot is involved with most projects from the earliest structural work on the building: this means that she can easily take into account small details that will be important during later stages.

This report showcases Benedikte Lecot's professional expertise: the contemporary classic design of a home in a timeless rustic style.

This extra-long corridor gives an overview of the two circulation axes: the ground floor and upstairs.

Rustic accents in this timeless home. The clean lines of an open fireplace in bluestone. The curtains harmonise with the colour of the walls.

p. 148-149
Oiled-white solid-oak floor. The high MDF skirting boards have been painted white. Work of art with artichoke by Ria de Henau.

The ceiling-height panelling has been painted using a stripe technique. The steel frame contains doors that open 180°. The floor is in aged bluestone.

The extra-wide oven is integrated into a ceiling-height wall-unit. The cooking island stands in a central position.

p. 154-155

Wooden chairs and a
painted bench around a
long refectory table.

The bathroom floor consists of old terracotta parfeuille tiles. Built-in washbasins and bath. The wooden shutters are made of painted MDF. The shower is fully clad in pale natural-stone tiles.

Shades of white and pink in this girls' bedroom.

BENEDIKTE LECOT
Interiors

MOB +32 (0)495 29 28 39
F +32 (0)51 32 07 28
www.b-lecot.be
interiors@b-lecot.be

A symbiosis of classic and contemporary in this office: a fitted carpet in a plain, warm shade and a classic armchair have been combined with an ultramodern artwork.

A boys' bedroom. An extra-long desk with a view of the garden.

SOBER REFINEMENT
IN A CLASSIC FRENCH MANOIR

This classic French manoir in the leafy outskirts of Antwerp was constructed by Coster-mans.

The company devoted the utmost attention to the selection of materials, installing un-usual antique tiles, durable old parquet floors, exceptional fireplaces and other special de-tails. The look is timeless, yet contemporary: a sober and sophisticated living environ-ment.

Calm, pale shades in the entrance hall with its French oak staircase with balusters and reclaimed floor with octagonal Burgundy tiles and square slate cabochons.

The sitting room with an old French oak parquet floor in Hungarian point.

The salon with its historic French Louis XV fireplace.

Natural materials have been combined with a bright green accent.

p. 168-169
The TV area has a bold,
yet successful, mix of
antique pieces and
modern designer
furniture (Vitra Classic
Lounge Chair and
Ottoman, designed by
Charles and Ray Eames).

165

A timeless, solid-oak kitchen in combination with a hand-painted pine table. The work surface is in a grey French natural stone. The cooker is the Provençal model from the French company Delaubrac. The wall tiles behind the cooker are hand-made Moroccan zeliges.

Various forms of ironwork: windows, dresser doors and the antique gate to the wine cellar.

COSTERMANS nv
Dwarsdreef 52
B – 2970 Schilde
T +32 (0)3 385 02 44
F +32 (0)3 384 29 66
www.costermans-projecten.be
info@costermans-projecten.be

A PASSION FOR MATERIALS WITH A HISTORY

Dirk Cousaert is a dedicated professional with a preference for time-honoured techniques and rough materials that have a history.

In his traditional carpenter's shop and stonemason's yard, the most exceptional kitchens, washbasins, tables, doors, and other items are created, all of which have sprung from the imagination of this constantly inspired artist and entrepreneur.

This report is a beautiful showcase of Cousaert – Van der Donckt's expert skill: this country house has been completely fitted out and furnished with creations by the company from the Flemish Ardennes.

The terrace table is made from exceedingly strong greenheart wood: a Class I variety of timber that was reclaimed from the harbour of Nieuwpoort. The oak wall cupboard and the side unit with its bluestone surface were also designed and created by Cousaert.
Bluestone terrace tiles.

A wine-tasting table in oak and Belgian bluestone.

The whole wall has been clad with oak planks. The sideboard has been partially incorporated into the wall; there is space for electrical cables above, and an alcove for the flat-screen television alongside.

p. 178
A robust coffee table, made from old wrought iron and sawn oak planks, which have been riveted together.

A bathroom with a built-in cupboard, washstand and wall unit, all made of old oak, as is the floor.

A two-seater bench made from oak and steel. Bluestone washbasin on an old-oak cupboard.

In the background, a section of a custom-built 'windmill staircase' by Cousaert – Van der Donckt.

One of Cousaert's brainwaves: an old iron workbench with a bluestone washbasin on top.

A spiral staircase that was made and installed by Cousaert.

COUSAERT – VAN DER DONCKT
Stationsstraat 160
B – 9690 Kluisbergen
T +32 (0)55 38 70 53
F +32 (0)55 38 60 39
www.cousaert-vanderdonckt.be
www.keuken-cuisine.be
info@cousaert-vanderdonckt.be
Open Monday, Tuesday and
Friday from 1 pm to 6 pm.
Saturday from 2 pm to 6 pm
and last Sunday of the month
from 2 pm to 6 pm.

Details of the bushhammered bluestone.

181

BLENDING
WITH THE LANDSCAPE

All of the elements of this project have blended into the surrounding natural land-scape: the old farmhouse that gives the impression of having been there for centuries, the two extensions (the garage and the kitchen), which were built by Heritage Buildings, and the garden, which merges perfectly with the rural surroundings.

The garage extension to the left of the main building was built years ago by Heritage Buildings.
The owners recently asked Heritage Buildings to extend the kitchen by adding a dining area, as the space had
become too small for an active family with two children.

The oak extension by Heritage Buildings blends
seamlessly with the garden. As soon as the
temperature outside allows, the doors are
opened wide.
Over time, the wooden planking outside has
gained a beautiful silver-grey patina.

Antique roof tiles emphasise the rustic
character of the house.

Ballmore is a recently founded gardening company. They run their own tree nursery, and also see to the design and planting of gardens that harmonise perfectly with the landscape. Ballmore usually put in more mature plants, such as the pear trees and the clumps of box shown here.

The large window provides a unique view over the expansive landscape.

Heritage Buildings transformed the kitchen space, originally a small area, into a fully fledged kitchen-cum-dining room. The oak structure is held together with mortise and tenon joints: there are no nails involved at all. The truss, open right up into the ridge of the roof, creates an authentic, rustic atmosphere.

The large windows provide a 180° view of the garden.

All of the pipes and cables have been concealed within the wooden interior planking.

p. 194

The oak arches harmonise with the large window sections.

Oak has been used throughout. The oak parquet floor
flows seamlessly into the oak-wood structure of the kitchen
and dining area.

HERITAGE BUILDINGS nv
    Ambiorixlei 8b
    B − 2900 Schoten
    T +32 (0)3 685 20 00
    F +32 (0)3 685 23 73
    www.heritagebuildings.be
    info@heritagebuildings.be

Garden design and creation:
BALLMORE
    Melkouwensteenweg 139
    B − 2590 Berlaar
    MOB +32 (0)477 66 34 84
    T/F +32 (0)15 25 36 70
    info@ballmore.com

ADDRESSES

b+ villas
Nieuwlandlaan 19
B – 3200 Aarschot
T +32 (0)16 56 79 31
F +32 (0)16 56 20 38
www.bplusvillas.be
info@bplusvillas.be
p. 120-133

b+ interiors
Nieuwlandlaan 19
B – 3200 Aarschot
T +32 (0)16 55 35 60
www.bplusinteriors.be
info@bplusinteriors.be
p. 120-133

HERITAGE BUILDINGS sa
Ambiorixlei 8b
B – 2900 Schoten
T +32 (0)3 685 20 00
F +32 (0)3 685 23 73
www.heritagebuildings.be
info@heritagebuildings.be
p. 182-197

BALLMORE
Design and contractors of gardens
Melkouwensteenweg 139
B – 2590 Berlaar
MOB +32 (0)477 66 34 84
T/F +32 (0)15 25 36 70
info@ballmore.com
p. 182-197

ANNICK COLLE
Interior architect
Reinaertdreef 8
B – 9830 Sint-Martens-Latem
T +32 (0)9 282 66 41
F +32 (0)9 281 18 57
p. 136-143

COSTERMANS VILLA-PROJECTEN sa
Dwarsdreef 52
B – 2970 Schilde
T +32 (0)3 385 02 44
F +32 (0)3 384 29 66
www.costermans-projecten.be
info@costermans-projecten.be
p. 160-175

COUSAERT – VAN DER DONCKT
Stationsstraat 160
B – 9690 Kluisbergen
T +32 (0)55 38 70 53
F +32 (0)55 38 60 39
www.cousaert-vanderdonckt.be
www.keuken-cuisine.be
info@cousaert-vanderdonckt.be
p. 176-181

BERNARD DE CLERCK
Architects sprl
Aarselestraat 26
B – 8700 Aarsele
T +32 (0)51 63 61 39
F +32 (0)51 63 52 15
info@bernarddeclerck.be
p. 80-95

DEJAEGERE sprl
Virginie & Odile Dejaegere
Grote Markt 7
B – 8500 Kortrijk
T +32 (0)56 22 87 81
F +32 (0)56 20 49 93
MOB +32 (0)475 79 13 78
www.dejaegere-interiors.be
info@dejaegere-interiors.be
Only after appointment
p. 96-107

DEMYTTENAERE H-C sprl
Architects
Koningslaan 160
B – 8300 Knokke-Heist
T +32 (0)50 62 37 79
F +32 (0)50 62 37 80
hcd@myth.be
p. 68-79

BENEDIKTE LECOT
Interiors
MOB +32 (0)495 29 28 39
F +32 (0)51 32 07 28
www.b-lecot.be
interiors@b-lecot.be
p. 144-159

SAND'S COMPANY
Interiors
T +32 (0)50 62 68 08
F +32 (0)50 62 37 80
p. 68-79

TRADIPLAN
Lodderstraat 14
B – 2880 Bornem
T +32 (0)3 889 15 75
F +32 (0)3 889 26 66
www.tradiplan.be
info@tradiplan.be
p. 108-119

VLASSAK-VERHULST sa
Moerstraat 53
B – 2970 's-Gravenwezel
T +32 (0)3 658 07 00
F +32 (0)3 658 46 45
www.vlassakverhulst.be
info@vlassakverhulst.be
p. 16-35 & 36-49

PUBLISHER

BETA-PLUS Publishing

Termuninck 3

B - 7850 Enghien (Belgium)

T. +32 (0)2 395 90 20

F. +32 (0)2 395 90 21

www.betaplus.com

betaplus@skynet.be

PHOTOGRAPHY

All pictures: Jo Pauwels, except:

p. 36-49: Jan Verlinde (and partially p. 182-197)

p. 144, 154-155, 157 above & 159: Claude Smekens

p. 176-181: Moniek Peers

GRAPHIC DESIGN

POLYDEM

Nathalie Binart

TRANSLATION

Laura Watkinson

January 2007

ISBN 13: 978 90 772 1364 3

ISBN 10: 90 772 1364 3